FOR

WITH

lots of kisses

FROM

FORBIDDEN KISS

KEITH LABAN

lots of kisses

WITH AN INTRODUCTION BY LISA TUTTLE

Paper Tiger

A Dragon's World Ltd Imprint

Dragon's World Ltd
Limpsfield
SURREY RH8 0DY
Great Britain

Designed by Julie and Steve Ridgeway, assisted by Frank Barron.

ISBN 0 905895 89 4

Printed in Italy

The Publishers wish to thank Chris Meiklejohn, of Meiklejohn Illustration, without whom this book would not have been possible.

Cover illustration by Syd Brak

KISSES

COVER GIRL KISS SYD BRAK
FORBIDDEN KISS KEITH LABAN
FIRST KISS PETE KELLY
FAIRYTALE KISS PETER NEAME
KISSES FOR SALE MARTIN GASCOIGNE
KISSING TIME ED STEWART
RELUCTANT KISS DAVID HOLMES
KISS AND MAKE UP KEITH LABAN
COMIC-STRIP KISS JOHN MAC
DRIVE-IN KISS BRIAN JAMES
REFLECTIVE KISS NIGEL TIDMAN
ELECTRIC KISS SYD BRAK
SPORTING KISS PHIL LITTLER
COMPUTER KISS ED STEWART
KOOL KATZ KISS ANDREW FARLEY
KISS AND TELL BRIAN JAMES
KISS ME KWICK GAVIN MACLEOD
EROTIC KISS SYD BRAK
SCREEN KISS JOHN MAC
COPYCAT KISS WARREN MADILL
SEDUCTIVE KISS GARETH WILLIAMS
SEALED WITH A KISS GERRY PRESTON
FOOLISH KISS IRVINE PEACOCK
COWBOY KISS WARREN MADILL
PRIMEVAL KISS JOHN MAC
CRINGING KISS WARREN MADILL
LONG - DISTANCE KISS SYD BRAK
SUN-KISSED DAVID HOLMES
INSTANT KISS PETE KELLY
WET KISS JEFF CUMMINGS
MERMAID KISS ANDREW FARLEY
PRINCELY KISS IRVINE PEACOCK
KISS OF DEATH SYD BRAK
COSMIC KISS PETE KELLY
CLASSIC KISS BARRY LEPARD
HOMECOMING KISS PAUL SIMMONS
FRENCH KISS ROGER PEARCE
FAREWELL KISS PAUL SIMMONS
ONE GREAT KISS FOR MANKIND BARRY LEPARD

INTRODUCTION
LISA TUTTLE

Who'd want a world without kisses?

Like art, alcohol and cooking, kissing is a luxury and a symbol of civilization which animals live quite happily without. Doubtless there are people who do the same, but to an orally-fixated person like myself, the idea is horrifying. Why, I'd sooner give up chocolate! Not necessary to survival, communication or reproduction, kissing is the gratuitous act which makes life so much more fun.

The kiss is the perfect symbol of love, the vivid emblem of romance. Even children understand it. Love is mysterious, but kisses are real.

Kissing is something anyone can do, at any age, in public or in private, for a variety of reasons. And you don't need a doctorate of kissology, or even a marriage certificate, to become an expert on the subject.

Sleeping Beauty was awakened, the Beast transformed, frog turned into prince, all through the magic of a kiss. The moral? Kisses change lives. And love without kisses is hardly love at all. Popular fiction, songs on the radio, movies, all repeat the same lesson.

As a child I called my pillow Freddy, held him in my arms and pressed my lips to his blank face, imagining he was kissing me back. I longed to know what my first kiss would feel like, and how it would happen. It looked so easy in comics and the movies, but in real life, I worried, wouldn't we bang our noses together? And what about bad breath? Or braces? What if the points of my fashionable, harlequin glasses jabbed him in the eye? Impossible to take them off first, to look as if I *expected* to be kissed, and I was much too short-sighted to leave them at home. And what about the boy? How would I recognize Mr Right? Would I know what to do when he put his arms around me?

My first kiss — my first dozen kisses — happened on my first date. I was thirteen, at home considered too young to go out with boys, but spending a week in the country with a friend, home restrictions didn't apply. Betty had a boyfriend, and he was enlisted to bring along someone for me. My first date! I can't even remember his name now, only that he was an "older man" — all of fifteen — with an East Texas twang to his voice, dark hair, and glasses.

Would he try to kiss me? From my researches on the subject, I knew he was supposed to try, and that I was not supposed to let him. But curiosity weakened me. Maybe I would let him. If he tried. How humiliating if he didn't. I worried at the problem while we sat in the local cinema, munching popcorn and watching *Dr. Zhivago*. Omar Sharif really knew how to kiss. If only I looked like Julie Christie.

After the movie the boys took us, not home, but out to Horseshoe Canyon, the popular parking spot. The two in the front seat sank out of sight and there came the unmistakable, plosive sound of lips meeting and parting.

I didn't know what to do, or where to look. To my relief, my date acted with all the *savoir faire* – if less passion – of an Omar Sharif who has discovered himself alone with Julie Christie in the back of a '59 Chevy.

First he took off his glasses and then, with the expertise of a licensed optician, removed mine. No subsequent undressing has ever seemed so fraught with tender possibility. Blind as moles, we move closer until our faces collided, and we kissed.

The world did not change. It did not even move. There were no explosions or transformations: I was not in love.

My first kiss may have lacked that essential spark, but later I realized that it doesn't matter how you begin, so long as you have faith and continue. I remained interested in the idea of kissing, although it was some years before I had the chance to kiss anyone other than the faithful Freddy.

I was in love with the next boy who kissed me, and what a difference it made! That was when I discovered for myself what the poets and songwriters had been saying all along – that kisses really *can* be more intoxicating than wine. I stopped worrying about bumping noses or locking braces: this was bliss.

Even in these more liberated times (does anyone still worry about the morality of kissing on a first date?) the kiss retains its allure. And not just as a symbol. Kisses can be all things to all people, as the artists represented in this book demonstrate. Powerful, erotic, shocking, tender, innocent, romantic, seductive, sweet, silly, enslaving, enchanting, enriching or just plain odd – there are as many possibilities in life as in art, and the choice is up to you.

"Bachelor's fare; bread and cheese, and kisses," said Jonathan Swift, and any true lover would agree. Who needs elaborate meals, wines, expensive gifts, when you have each other? Love will survive the lack of any luxury – except kisses. And they're the best bargain around. Everyone can afford to give them, and everyone loves receiving them. So splurge! Give the one you love lots and lots of kisses, and don't be surprised when you get them all back.

FIRST KISS

PETE KELLY

FAIRYTALE KISS
PETER NEAME

KISSES FOR SALE

MARTIN GASCOIGNE

KISSING TIME

ED STEWART

RELUCTANT KISS

DAVID HOLMES

KISS AND MAKE UP

KEITH LABAN

COMIC-STRIP KISS

JOHN MAC

DRIVE-IN KISS

BRIAN JAMES

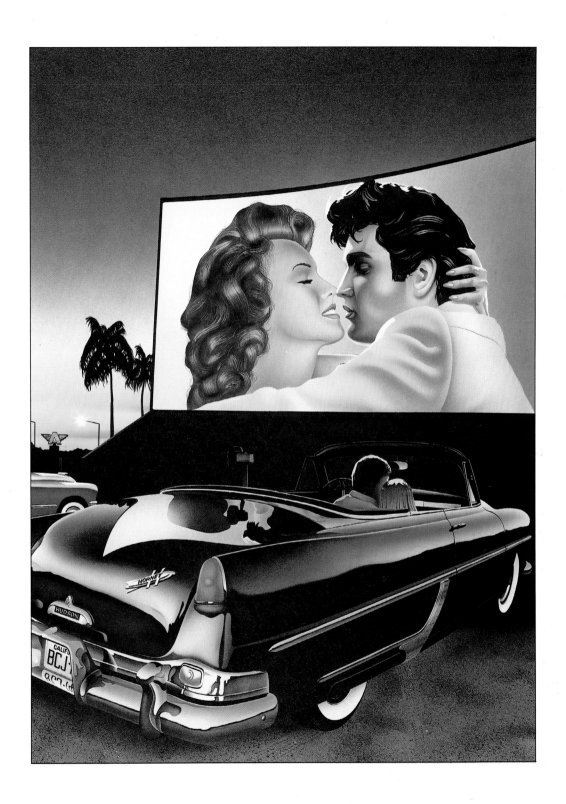

REFLECTIVE KISS
NIGEL TIDMAN

ELECTRIC KISS

SYD BRAK

SPORTING KISS

PHIL LITTLER

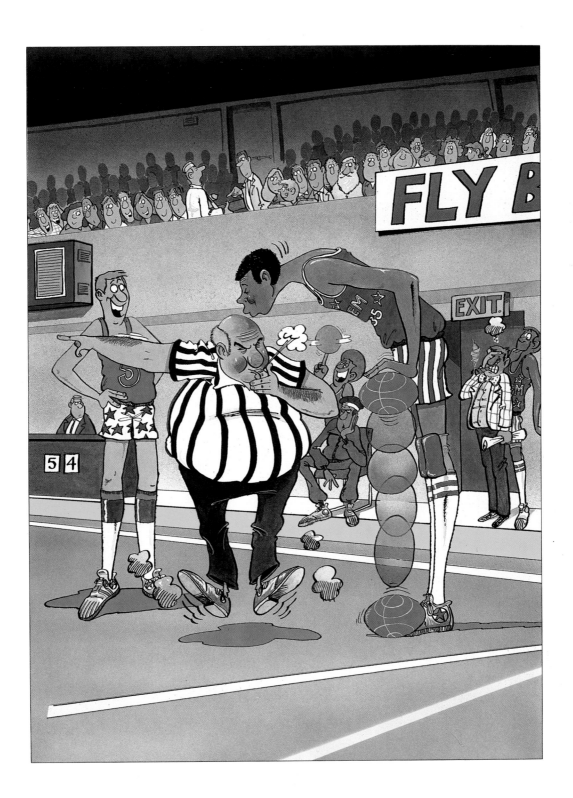

COMPUTER KISS

ED STEWART

KOOL KATZ KISS

ANDREW FARLEY

KISS 'N' TELL

BRIAN JAMES

KISS ME KWICK

GAVIN MACLEOD

EROTIC KISS

SYD BRAK

SCREEN KISS

JOHN MAC

COPYCAT KISS

WARREN MADILL

SEDUCTIVE KISS

GARETH WILLIAMS

SEALED WITH A KISS

GERRY PRESTON

FOOLISH KISS

IRVINE PEACOCK

Warren Madill

PRIMEVAL KISS

JOHN MAC

CRINGING KISS

WARREN MADILL

LONG DISTANCE KISS

SUN-KISSED

DAVID HOLMES

INSTANT KISS

PETE KELLY

WET KISS

JEFF CUMMINS

MERMAID KISS

ANDREW FARLEY

PRINCELY KISS

IRVINE PEACOCK

COSMIC KISS

PETE KELLY

CLASSIC KISS

BARRY LEPARD

HOMECOMING KISS

PAUL SIMMONS

FRENCH KISS

ROGER PEARCE

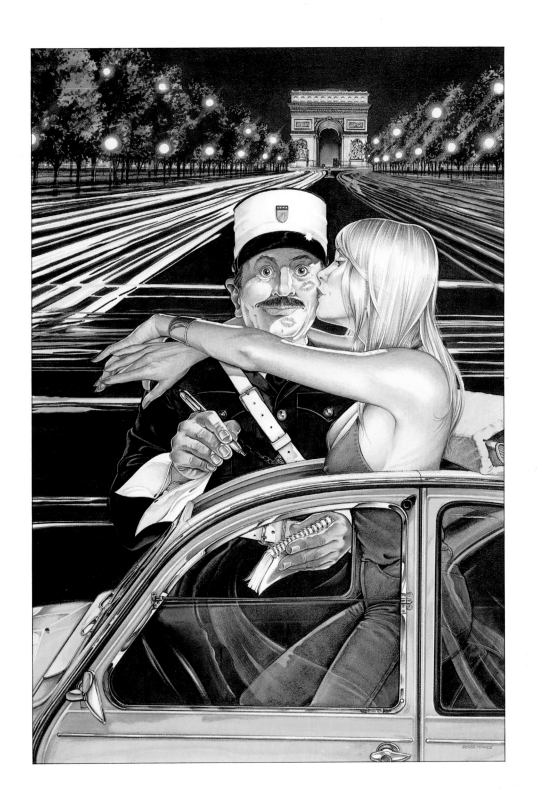

FAREWELL KISS

PAUL SIMMONS